GET INTO SMOOTHIES

GET-INTO-IT GUIDES

JAIME WINTERS

CRABTREE
Publishing Company
www.crabtreebooks.com

GET-INTO-IT GUIDES

Author: Jaime Winters

Editors: Marcia Abramson, Philip Gebhardt

Photo research: Melissa McClellan

Editorial director: Kathy Middleton

Proofreader: Janine Deschenes

Cover/Interior Design: T.J. Choleva

**Production coordinator and
 Prepress technician:** Samara Parent

Print coordinator: Margaret Amy Salter

Consultant: Karen O'Connor
Executive Chef at Daniel *et* Daniel, Toronto, the
2015 winner of the The International Caterers
Association, CATIE Chef of the Year Award.

Project Designers: Diorama on page 22 – Joshua
Avramson; diorama on page 24 – Melissa
McClellan; models on pages 26, 28 – Janet
Compare-Fritz

Developed and produced for Crabtree Publishing
by BlueApple*Works* Inc.

Photographs

Shutterstock.com: © Aleksandar Mijatovic (cover top banner); © photogal (cover bottom middle);
© Funny Solution Studio (cover center right); © AHATHIR MOHD YASIN (cover center left);
© photokin (cover top left); © mama_mia (cover left 3rd from top); © Darkkong (cover left 2cd from
top); © govindji (cover bottom left); © Volosina (cover top right); © Es75 (c0ver far right); © MaraZe
(title page); © merc67 (TOC background); © photka (p. 4); © Alena Ozerova (p. 5); © bitt24 (p. 6 top);
© PHILIPIMAGE (p. 6 middle); © sunabesyou (p. 6 bottom, 10); © Ravennka (p. 6, 10 background);
© monticello (p. 7 top); © Africa Studio (p. 7 2cd from top); © alexpro9500o (p. 7 3rd from top);
© nehopelon (p. 7 bottom); © RoyStudioEU (p.9 bottom); p. 12 top, left to right © Titus and Co,
© Darryl Brooks, © Letterberry, © exopixel, © Brent Hofacker, © Nanette Grebe; p. 12 middle, left to
right © Subbotina Anna, © stockphoto-graf, © ChameleonsEye, © Africa Studio, © Africa Studio,
© BW Folsom; p. 13 top, left to right © Brent Hofacker, © Africa Studio, © JeniFoto, © Zigzag Mountain
Art, © TalyaAL, © Oksana Mizina, © George Dolgikh, © Melica; p. 13 middle, left to right © Tim UR,
© MSPhotographic, © Ekaterina Kondratova, © julie deshaies, © Christian Jung, © Jen Petrie,
© goldenjack, © Avelina; © Nattika (p. 14 top left); © leonori (p. 14 top right, p. 15 page top); © matin
(p. 14 middle right, back cover middle bottom); © Maks Narodenko (p. 14 bottom right); © 5PH (p. 15
top left); © A. Laengauer (p. 15 top right); © Maks Narodenko (p. 15 middle left); © Roman Samokhin
(p. 15 middle right); © Tadeusz Wejkszo (p. 15 bottom); © Kovaleva_Ka (p. 16 top Left); © Elena
Schweitzerp (p. 17 page top); © AN NGUYEN (p. 17 top left, 23 top); © Volosina (p. 17 bottom left, back
cover top right); © Imageman (p. 17 bottom left); © Binh Thanh Bui (p. 18 top left, 18 middle right, 19
middle left); © yurchello108 (p. 18 middle left); © Teri Virbickis (p. 18 top right); © JIANG HONGYAN
(p. 18 bottom right); © Lightspring (p. 19 page top); © eleginatania (p. 19 top left); © Barbara Dudzinska
(p. 19 top right); © Tim UR (p. 19 middle); © NIPAPORN PANYACHAROEN (p. 19 bottom left);
© MAHATHIR MOHD YASIN (p. 19 bottom right); © Volosina (p. 21 top left); © Anna_Pustynnikova
(p. 21 bottom left); © Ildiko Szanto (p. 23 middle); © Kovaleva_Ka (p. 24 top); © baibaz (p. 25 top right,
back cover middle); © stockphoto-grafz (p. 25 top left); © baibaz (p. 25 bottom middle); © Tadeusz
Wejkszo (p. 25 page bottom); Barbara Neveu (p. 25 bottom right); Stepanek Photography (p. 26 bottom
left); © Liliya Kandrashevich (p. 26 top, back cover top left); © JeniFoto (p. 29 top); © Abramova Elena
(p. 29 top left);

© Austen Photography TOC, p. 4 left, 9, 13 bottom, 14 bottom left, 16 bottom left, 17 yop right, p. 18 left,
20 top, 21 bottom right, 22, 23 bottom, 25 middle, 27, 28;

© Molly Klager (p. 8, 11, 12 bottom, 20 bottom, 24 bottom, 29 middle, 29 bottom, back cover

Library and Archives Canada Cataloguing in Publication

Winters, Jaime, author
 Get into smoothies / Jaime Winters.

(Get-into-it guides)
Includes index.
Issued in print and electronic formats.
ISBN 978-0-7787-3403-1 (hardcover).—
ISBN 978-0-7787-3407-9 (softcover).--
ISBN 978-1-4271-1916-2 (HTML)

 1. Smoothies (Beverages)--Juvenile literature. 2. Cookbooks. I. Title.

TX817.S636W56 2017   j641.2'6   C2016-907388-2
                                                C2016-907389-0

Library of Congress Cataloging-in-Publication Data

Names: Winters, Jaime, author.
Title: Get into smoothies / Jaime Winters.
Description: New York : Crabtree Publishing Company, [2017] | Series:
 Get-into-it guides | Includes index.
Identifiers: LCCN 2017000360 (print) | LCCN 2017001593 (ebook) | ISBN
 9780778734031 (reinforced library binding : alk. paper) | ISBN
 9780778734079 (pbk. : alk. paper) | ISBN 9781427119162 (Electronic HTML)
Subjects: LCSH: Smoothies (Beverages)--Juvenile literature. | LCGFT:
 Cookbooks.
Classification: LCC TX817.S636 W56 2017 (print) | LCC TX817.S636 (ebook) |
 DDC 641.8/75--dc23
LC record available at https://lccn.loc.gov/2017000360

Crabtree Publishing Company
www.crabtreebooks.com   1-800-387-7650

Printed in Canada/032017/BF20170111

**Published in Canada
Crabtree Publishing**
616 Welland Ave.
St. Catharines, Ontario
L2M 5V6

**Published in the United States
Crabtree Publishing**
PMB 59051
350 Fifth Avenue, 59th Floor
New York, New York 10118

**Published in the United Kingdom
Crabtree Publishing**
Maritime House
Basin Road North, Hove
BN41 1WR

**Published in Australia
Crabtree Publishing**
3 Charles Street
Coburg North
VIC, 3058

CONTENTS

SMOOTH AND DELICIOUS DRINKS

Mmm…mmm…slurp! Crushed fruit drinks were tasty chug-a-lugs in the Mediterranean, Asia, and Latin America hundreds of years ago. But they didn't take off around the world until the blender was invented in the 1930s. The blender could crush, mix, and blend whole fruits and vegetables like never before. The inventor of the blender, Fred Waring, was right when he said it would "revolutionize" drinks. Not only did it break down fruits and vegetables so people could absorb the **nutrients** better, it also whipped them into smooth drinks. In the 1960s, a health food movement swept North America, and "smoothies" began popping up at California beaches, health food stores, and restaurants.

Many different cultures have their own versions of smoothies. Other popular blended drinks include the mango lassi in India and the jallab in the Middle East.

NUTRITION IN A GLASS

Just suck it up! Chances are you won't find a drink as delicious and nutritious as a smoothie. Made of whole fruits and vegetables, smoothies are brimming with water, **antioxidants**, **fiber**, and nutrients, such as **vitamins**, **minerals**, **enzymes**, and **phytonutrients**. Nutrients like these often work together as a team. This makes eating or drinking whole fruits and vegetables better than taking vitamins and nutrient pills, or supplements. Since you swallow all the "team players" in one shot, they can get the nutritional job done. What's more, the fiber in whole fruits and vegetables helps keep your blood sugar stable, lowers **cholesterol**, and gets rid of waste and deadly toxins.

How to Use This Book

The ideas for smoothies in this book are meant to inspire you to create your own recipes and drinks. You can follow the steps provided, or use your imagination to create your own delicious drinks.

THE "VITAL" IN VITAMINS AND MINERALS

Vitamin A is key to healthy skin and hair as well as bone and tooth growth. It helps your vision and boosts your immune system.

Vitamin B2 converts food into energy, develops healthy skin, hair, and nails, and helps make cells and red blood cells.

Vitamin B6 boosts your immune system and helps you absorb **protein** as well as make cells and red blood cells.

Vitamin C helps protect body tissue from damage, fights infection, strengthens bones and teeth, and helps you absorb iron.

Vitamin E helps make red blood cells, balances cholesterol, and helps heal skin tissues.

Vitamin K helps blood clot, or stop bleeding, and helps your bones stay healthy.

Magnesium helps strengthen bones and teeth, promotes new cell growth, increases energy, and helps your body use B and C vitamins as well as calcium.

Manganese helps keep your bones, tissues, and nerves healthy and protects cells from damage by **free radicals**.

Potassium helps you stay hydrated, absorb nutrients, and keep a healthy heart.

Phosphorus boosts energy and helps keep your bones, teeth, and nerves healthy.

NUTRITION MATTERS

Whether you want to play, look, or feel your best, proper nutrition is essential. Just ask any pro athlete. Take the football players on the New York Giants, for example. The Giants work with a nutritionist, Tara Ostrowe, to make sure they get the nutrients they need for peak performance.

Eating a balanced diet is the key to staying healthy both mentally and physically.

Tara includes smoothies as a way to achieve this. For your body to grow and develop, you need the same nutrients as top athletes—vitamins, minerals, proteins, **carbohydrates**, and fats. The only difference is that you need different amounts of them than the athletes. And don't think you can stop eating them once you're a grown-up. The fact is, we need nutrients all our lives.

WATER—THE DRINK OF LIFE

You cannot survive without water. Your body is made of cells and every single one of them needs water to work. Your body uses water to keep a steady temperature, get rid of waste, and "grease" your joints to move easily. In fact, more than half of your body weight is made up of water! You can't survive for more than a few days without it. It's important to make sure you are drinking enough water so your body keeps working properly. Make sure to drink water when you're thirsty and drink extra water when you are exercising or when it's warm.

Lots of foods contain water, too. 80 to 95 percent of a whole fruit or vegetable is water. The other 5 to 20 percent is carbohydrates, fiber, and nutrients.

FOOD GUIDES

To make sure you eat a healthy diet, check out the United States Department of Agriculture (USDA) and the Canada Food Guide dietary recommendations. They are designed to help you eat healthy. See links to websites on page 30. They divide food into different groups. They also recommend the amount of food to eat from each group every day.

USDA's *MyPlate* Guide

MyPlate puts together healthy meals from five main food groups: fruits, vegetables, grains, protein foods, and dairy. Half the plate should be fruits and vegetables, and half should be grains and proteins.

○ Vegetables: Veggies are a big part of *MyPlate*. They can be fresh, canned, frozen, or juiced. Just make sure the juice is 100% vegetables.

○ Fruits: Like veggies, fruits can be fresh, canned, frozen, or 100% juice. Also like veggies, they come in lots of shapes and colors.

○ Grains: Cereal, bread, and other grain products are made from wheat, oats, rice, barley, and corn. Whole grains are best because they contain more nutrients and fiber.

○ Protein foods: Animal proteins are meat, poultry, seafood, and eggs. Vegetarian proteins are soy products, beans, peas, nuts, and seeds. A healthy diet can be based on either type of protein, or both.

○ Dairy: To be part of this group, products must have a good calcium content. Milk, cheese, yogurt, soy milk, and even ice cream count as dairy, but butter, cream, and cream cheese with little or no calcium do not. Most dairy group choices should be fat-free or low-fat.

CANADA FOOD GUIDE

According to the Canada Food Guide, kids from 9 to 13 years of age should eat the following number of servings from four food groups:

Vegetables and fruit – 6 servings a day

Grain products, such as bread, rice, pasta, cereal – 6 servings a day

Milk and alternatives, such as soy or almond milk, cheese, yogurt, kefir – 3–4 servings a day

Meat and alternatives, such as fish, tofu, eggs, peanut or nut butters, legumes, seeds, nuts – 1-2 servings a day

USING A BLENDER

When it comes to making a smoothie, a blender's got the right stuff. It's the whirling action of the blades in a blender that turns solid food into thick liquid drinks. You need an upright blender—one with a container on top—not a handheld stick blender because it isn't made for blending fruits, vegetables, or ice. High-performance upright blenders, which usually have a steel base, glass container, and powerful motor, work best. But don't worry. You can still make smoothies with a low-performance one.

Cleaning your blender

For smooth and easy cleaning, fill your blender with warm water and a squirt of liquid dish soap and let it sit for a while.

USING A LOW-PERFORMANCE BLENDER

The key to using this type of blender is the order in which you add the ingredients. Follow the order listed in How to Blend a Smoothie on page 9 for best results. All the recipes in this book list ingredients in this order. You might also need to grate fruits and vegetables, or chop them into smaller pieces, as well as stop the blender and stir the mixture a few times to blend it smoothly. Adding a bit more liquid might also help to get the **consistency** you want.

USING A HIGH-PERFORMANCE BLENDER

Some high performance blenders have smoothie and ice crushing buttons. First, use the smoothie button to cut and liquefy fresh fruits and vegetables. Then add any frozen fruit or ice and use the ice button. Finally, use the blend button to give your drink a smooth finish. If your blender doesn't have these buttons, throw in all the non-frozen ingredients and start to blend at low-speed and gradually move to high-speed. Then add any frozen items and blend again.

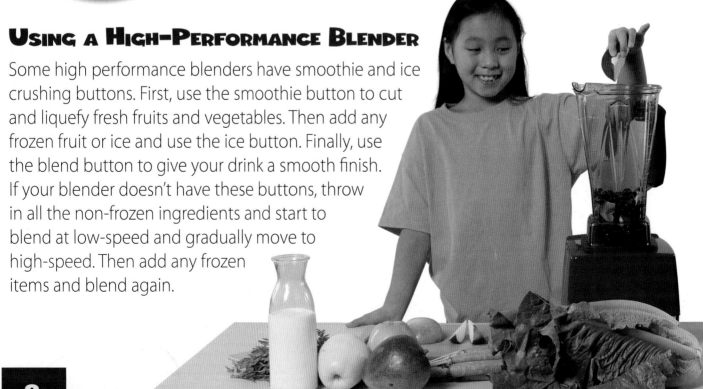

HOW TO BLEND A SMOOTHIE

Anyone can learn how to make healthy and delicious smoothies. Once you get the basics down, you'll be creating smoothies like a master in no time.

6 Nut or Soy Butter
Add any nut or soy butter last to help stop it from sticking to the sides of the blender. Blend again.

3 Fruits and Vegetables
Add any fresh fruits and veggies next. If you want a "creamy" consistency, add at least one banana, mango, peach, pear, apple, papaya, or avocado.

5 Frozen Stuff
Add any frozen fruit, vegetables, or ice cubes and blend again.

2 Powders and Seeds
Add any powdered ingredients, such as ground spices and protein powder, and seeds directly into the liquid to help blend them smoothly.

4 Leafy Greens
Add any leafy greens, such as spinach, on top and blend until smooth.

1 Liquids
Always pour them into the blender first. They're the base of all smoothies.

Making It Smooth
Can you sip your smoothie through a straw? If not, you may want to blend it longer or add a bit more liquid.

PROTEIN POWER

Proteins play a critical role in the human body. All your skin, hair, muscles, bones, and cells are made of proteins. They also repair body parts, produce energy, and control your body's **metabolism**—the key processes that keep your "engine" running. For a protein boost, add protein powder or some of these protein-rich foods to your smoothies: nuts, oats, seeds, tofu, or yogurt. Go to page 21 to learn more about each protein booster.

PREP WORK

You Will Need:
- Ingredients
- Large bowl
- Water
- ¼ cup (60 ml) of vinegar
- Vegetable brush
- Clean towel
- Knife
- Apple corer

You don't have to be a world-class chef to make smoothies. You don't even need to know how to cook a thing. Smoothies are a snap to whip up. Just follow the steps, methods, and tips below.

PICK THE BASE FOR YOUR SMOOTHIE

What puts the "smooth" in a smoothie? Liquids! Not only do liquids flow easily and fit the shape of any container, but you can't blend a smoothie without them. Liquids smooth the way for the blades of the blender to spin easily and the ingredients to mix together well. Liquids also load smoothies with flavor and nutrients. A variety of liquids such as water, coconut milk, fruit juice, vegetable juice, and milk make good bases for smoothies.

Base Tip

Even though yogurt is a semisolid, it's liquid-like enough to be a good base for smoothies.

MILK ALTERNATIVES

Some people cannot easily digest **lactose**, a natural sugar in cow's milk. They have **lactose intolerance** and often avoid foods made with cow's milk. Other people, such as **vegans** (see below), avoid cow's milk for other reasons. The good news is that several non-dairy milks, such as soy milk, almond milk, cashew milk, rice milk, and coconut milk can be substituted for cow's milk in smoothies.

Coconut Milk Tip

Coconut milk is a drink sold in cartons—not the canned coconut milk used in cooking. Made of coconut milk and water, it adds a light coconut flavor to smoothies.

I'M A VEGAN!

Being a vegan is a way of life. Vegans choose not to eat or use animal products in order to avoid cruelty to animals. That means vegans don't eat meat, fish, or eggs. Vegans don't drink milk and don't eat cheese or honey. They don't wear leather—jackets, belts, shoes, or any other leather doodads. And vegans don't use products that are tested on animals.

 Vegan smoothies in this book are marked with the V-Sign.

PREPPING MAIN INGREDIENTS

Peeling Challenge
Can you peel an orange so that the peel comes off in one unbroken piece? How about an apple?

WASH YOUR FRUITS AND VEGGIES

Raw fruits and veggies— the main ingredients—need to be washed well to remove dirt, **pesticides**, and other things. Fill a large bowl or sink with a mixture of water and vinegar. Use approximately one part of vinegar for every three parts of water. Place the fruits or veggies in the mixture, let them soak for a few minutes, and then wash them gently with your hands or a soft vegetable brush. Rinse them with water and pat dry with a clean towel.

PEELING, CHOPPING, AND CORING

Prep whole fruits and vegetables for smooth blending in your blender. Use a vegetable peeler to peel fruits and vegetables, a plastic knife to chop soft fruits such as bananas, and a metal knife to chop hard fruits and vegetables such as apples and carrots. Ask an adult to help you with the metal knife and follow the prep steps for different fruits and vegetables on pages 12–13.

PEELING APPLES

You can use a vegetable peeler to remove the skin from apples. Start at the top of the apple and circle down around the apple.

CORING APPLES

Ask an adult to help you use an apple corer to core an apple. Place the corer on top of the apple and push down, then twist and remove the core.

CHOPPING

Make sure to chop vegetables on a plastic or wooden cutting board. Hold the vegetable with one hand and cut chunks off. Take care to keep your fingers away from the cutting edge of the knife.

PREPPING WHOLE FRUITS AND VEGETABLES

Apples
Peel if desired. Remove the core and seeds with an apple corer. Cut into chunks.

Lemons, limes, and oranges
Remove the peel. Break into sections and remove the seeds. Use a knife to slit the skin and gently nudge out the seeds.

Bananas
Peel and break or slice into a few chunks. If frozen, thaw for five minutes, then peel and cut into chunks.

Safety Tip
Don't eat apple seeds. They're toxic. If they combine with enzymes in your gut, they can make deadly hydrogen cyanide. The good news is you would have to eat hundreds of seeds for them to act as a deadly poison."

Peaches
Peel the skin if desired, remove the pits, and cut into chunks.

Broccoli
Cut into florets by cutting off the stems from the "flowery tops."

Blueberries, blackberries, strawberries, raspberries
Wash and leave whole.

PEELING VEGETABLES

You will be able to peel veggies faster if you use a flat peeler instead of a traditional vertical peeler. Rest the tip of the vegetable on the cutting board. Hold the vegetable at a slight angle with one hand. Quickly and smoothly run the peeler from the top of the vegetable to the bottom. Turn the vegetable as you peel.

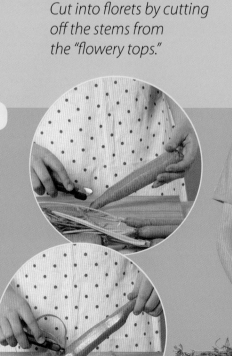

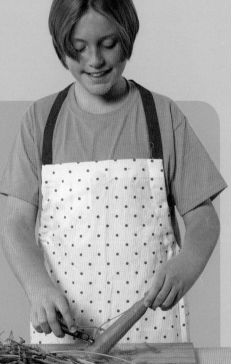

Cucumbers
Peel and cut into 4 or 5 chunks.

Kale
Remove the center ribs by tearing off the leaves.

Beets
Peel and chop into 1-inch (2.5 cm) chunks.

Carrots
Peel if desired and chop into 1-inch (2.5 cm) chunks.

Celery
Cut into 1-inch (2.5 cm) pieces.

Lettuce
Tear into shreds.

Kiwi
Peel and cut into several chunks.

Sweet Potatoes
Peel and cut into 1-inch (2.5 cm) chunks.

PREPPING MANGO

> **Safety Tip**
> Use a sturdy plastic knife or have an adult slice the mango.

On both sides of the pit, use a knife to slice the fruit from top to bottom all the way around the pit.

Separate the halves and remove the pit.

Without cutting through the skin, cut a checkerboard pattern into the flesh of both halves.

Around the edges, cut between the flesh and skin.

Use your thumbs to turn the flesh inside out, so the mango "cubes" pop out.

Then use a spoon to scoop out the cubes.

GOODNESS IN FRUITS

Nothing can refuel, recharge, and reboot your energy like a fruit smoothie. Fruits fuel your body with natural sugar and they don't take much time or energy to digest. As if that's not enough, fruits also contain fiber and acids—malic acid, citric acid, and tartaric acid—that work like cleansers. Tartaric acid helps you expel poop. Likewise, the antiseptic power of malic acid cleans and protects your gut, kidneys, liver, and stomach. What's more, malic acid tops up your energy and muscle power and can even clear your mind.

Raspberries are like nature's candy. Not only are they round and red, but they're also sweet and juicy. Raspberries are jam-packed with antioxidants and rich in vitamins C and K, manganese, and fiber.

Blueberries are a star ingredient of smoothies. Per serving, they're loaded with more antioxidants than most fruits or vegetables and are a good source of vitamins K and C and manganese. What's more, the flavor of blueberries goes with almost any fruit or nut.

Strawberries hit the sweet spot like no other. They're the world's most popular berries—and are near the top fruit source of vitamin C. That's not all. Strawberries are rich in manganese, fiber, and iodine.

TRY THIS!

Tutti Frutti Fuel

You Will Need:

- ½ cup (125 ml) orange juice
- ¼ cup (60 ml) water
- 1 cup (250 ml) seedless grapes
- 1 cup (250 ml) chopped cantaloupe
- ½ cup (125 ml) fresh or frozen berries

Put all ingredients in a blender and blend until smooth.

Fruit Tip

You can replace fresh fruit with frozen fruit and vice versa in smoothies. Just remember that frozen fruit not only chills the results but thickens them, too.

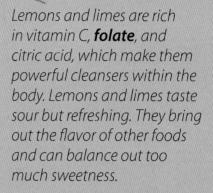

Grapes deliver a good dose of vitamins K and B2 and copper. They're rich in tartaric acid, which helps expel poop, and are an excellent source of phytonutrients, some of which may help humans live longer. Their sweet and tart flavor gives smoothies zing.

Lemons and limes are rich in vitamin C, **folate**, and citric acid, which make them powerful cleansers within the body. Lemons and limes taste sour but refreshing. They bring out the flavor of other foods and can balance out too much sweetness.

Apples have lots of malic acid to cleanse your body and amp up your energy. They're a great source of antioxidants, vitamin C, and fiber, and they've got enough flavor to make vegetable smoothies tastier for picky taste buds. Eating one a day might indeed keep the doctor away!

Mangoes pack a sweet and creamy punch of more than 20 vitamins and minerals—especially vitamins A, B6, C, and E, potassium, magnesium, phosphorus, and calcium— and they have lots of fiber. Some studies show that mangoes are helpful for healthy skin, hair, and fingernails.

Bananas are high in vitamins B6 and C, magnesium, and potassium. Their sweet, mashable flesh makes them perfect for sweetening and thickening smoothies. Use underripe, green, slightly yellow bananas if you don't want to add much banana flavor, or ripe, brown, yellow bananas if you want a stronger flavor.

Banana Tip

Frozen bananas give smoothies a thick creamy texture. To freeze underripe bananas, peel and bag them, squeeze out the air, and toss the sealed bag in the freezer. To freeze ripe brown bananas, just toss 'em in the freezer—peel and all.

VEGETABLES AND NUTS

Need to eat more vegetables? Who doesn't? Studies show that most people don't eat enough veggies. But if you toss them into a smoothie, you can drink vegetables instead—and they'll taste delicious. Or you might not even taste them at all! Not only will you boost your intake of veggies, but you'll also increase the nutrients you absorb. That's because raw veggies retain nutrients that are destroyed when vegetables are cooked. If vegetable smoothies are new to you, try adding mild-tasting veggies, such as romaine lettuce, celery, cucumbers, and carrots to your favorite fruit smoothies first. And for a nutty twist of flavor and protein, add nuts.

If the thought of drinking veggies makes you think "Eww," start with beets. Their sweet, earthy flavor pairs well not only with strawberries, bananas, and pineapple, but also with Boston lettuce, romaine lettuce, and spinach. What's more, they can color your smoothie red or purple!

Carrots add natural sweetness to smoothies. They're high in vitamins A, B1, B2, B6, C, E, and K as well as folate, biotin, potassium, manganese, and copper.

So what if eating asparagus might turn your pee green? The tender juicy spears are a great source of vitamins K, C, A, B2, and E, folate, copper, potassium, fiber, and protein. Combine them with fruit and other sweet flavors in a smoothie and you might not even know they're there.

TRY THIS!

"Beetlicious" Strawberry Blast
You Will Need: (V)

- 2¼ cups (560 ml) coconut milk
- 3 cups (750 ml) frozen strawberries
- 1 raw beet, peeled and sliced

Combine all ingredients in a blender and blend until smooth.

Veggie Tip

Want to make a vegetable smoothie taste out of this world? Add apples, grapes, or mangoes for a shot of flavor.

Sweet potatoes make smoothies creamy and are a good substitute for carrots, mangoes, or peaches in your recipe faves. Just peel them, chop or grate them, and throw them into your blender for a high dose of energy-boosting carbohydrates, vitamins A and C, fiber, potassium, and iron. Frozen chunks work well, too.

TRY THIS!

Sweet Potato Pick-Me-Up

You Will Need:

- 1 cup (250 ml) almond milk
- ½ teaspoon (2.5 ml) cinnamon
- ½ teaspoon (2.5 ml) allspice
- ½ cup (125 ml) sweet potato, grated
- 1 orange, peeled
- 2 tablespoons (30 ml) pecans
- 1 cup (250 ml) ice

Put all ingredients but the ice in a blender and blend until smooth. Add the ice and blend again until smooth.

HOW ABOUT SOME NUTS?

A handful of nuts makes the protein go down! Adding nuts to a smoothie gives you a nutty-tasting fix of protein, antioxidants, fiber, and a wide range of vitamins and minerals. Almonds, cashews, pecans, walnuts, and other tree nuts are stuffed with these nutrients, because they're seeds.

Even though peanuts are not nuts (they're legumes like lentils, peas, and beans), they're packed with similar nutrients. So they're grouped with nuts as a protein food source.

Food for Thought

Did you know peanuts are also called goobers? Peanuts have many names around the world. Goobers, one of the most popular ones, comes from the Bantu name for peanuts, nguba.

NUT ALLERGIES

Not everybody is nuts for nuts. Allergies to tree nuts—almonds, cashews, pecans, walnuts, and more—and peanuts are common. Chances are you know someone who's allergic to one or more tree nuts, peanuts, or even tree nuts and peanuts. What's more, if someone's allergic to one nut, they're more likely to be allergic to others. That's tough. Allergic reactions to nuts include swelling of the face, lips, and eyes, breaking out in hives or welts, tingling in the mouth, stomach pain, and vomiting. So it's best for people with a nut allergy to avoid tree nuts and peanuts altogether. That includes not eating them and not touching them or anything made with them.

LEAFY POWERHOUSES

A smoothie is only as healthy as its ingredients. Green vegetables—raw, green leafy ones such as kale, spinach, broccoli, Swiss chard, parsley, celery, or Romaine lettuce—usually make up about 40 percent of a green smoothie. The rest is mostly fruit. Green smoothies are not only high in nutrients, vitamins, and fiber, but they can also make almost any vegetable you don't like taste great. The secret behind blending the perfect green smoothie is using sweet fruits or even seeds to make your drink taste scrumptious.

Kale is very nutritious. It is stuffed with 45 different **flavonoids**, *packed with antioxidants, and full of fiber. Kale is also a very good source of vitamins A, C, K, and B6.*

Spinach is a good source of dietary fiber, protein, and vitamins K, A, C, E, and B6.

Broccoli is a good source of calcium and a very good source of vitamins A, C, and B6. Adding banana with broccoli helps to sweeten the taste and gives it the right amount of creaminess.

TRY THIS!

Kale Smoothie with Pineapple and Banana

You Will Need:

- ½ cup (125 ml) coconut milk
- 2 cups (500 ml) chopped kale
- 1½ cups (375 ml) chopped pineapple
- 1 ripe banana, chopped

(V)

Combine the ingredients in a blender and blend until smooth, about 1 minute, adding water to reach the desired consistency.

Kale Tip

Freeze your kale before using it. Even if it's only half frozen, the kale will taste less bitter. Wash the kale in the mixture of vinegar and water, de-rib it, and store it in the freezer, then grab as much as you want and throw it right into your blender for a quick, healthy drink.

Swiss chard is a very good source of vitamins A, C, E, K, and B6. Swiss chard tastes great with fruits such as bananas, pineapples, oranges, and even apples or pears.

A few fresh leaves of basil adds zest to green smoothies and a powerful dose of vitamin K, manganese, copper, and vitamins A and C.

Celery is a great addition to your green smoothies because it can help reduce the sweetness of a smoothie that is just too sweet. It is a good source of vitamins A, C, K, and B6.

Romaine lettuce has a mild flavor that is easily masked by fruit. You can add an entire head of lettuce to a fruit smoothie and not change the taste at all. It is also a good source of vitamins A, C, K, and several B vitamins.

Cucumbers add a crisp, refreshing flavor to fruit and green smoothies. All types of cucumbers are a good source of vitamins C and A.

TRY THIS!

Spinach Smoothie with Celery, Cucumber, and Lemon

You Will Need: Ⓥ

- ☐ 1 medium celery stalk, sliced
- ☐ ½ medium cucumber, sliced
- ☐ 2 tablespoons (30 ml) lemon juice
- ☐ 1 cup (250 ml) baby spinach
- ☐ water to maximum line on your blender

Place the celery, cucumber, lemon juice, spinach, and water in a blender. Blend for about 1 minute or until the mixture becomes smooth.

BREAKFAST SMOOTHIES

When you need to get up and go, downing a breakfast smoothie is the perfect way to fuel up. Some breakfast smoothies can top up your morning meal with a blast of tutti-frutti, veggi-rutti vitamins and minerals. Others are your morning meal in a glass, delivering enough nutrient-and-protein pep to keep you going until lunch. And if making a smoothie first thing in the morning scrambles your brains, don't worry. You can do any prep work—washing, peeling, or chopping—the night before, so your ingredients are ready to blend, whip, and sip.

BANANARAMA BRAIN BOOST

You Will Need:

- ½ cup (125 ml) milk
- 1 tablespoon (15 ml) ground flaxseed
- 2 ripe bananas
- 1 cup (250 ml) fresh or frozen blueberries
- ¾ cup (180 ml) plain yogurt

Makes 2 servings.

Drink this breakfast in a glass for a bananarama blast of brainpower.

1. *Peel the bananas and break each in half.*

2. *Put the milk, flaxseed, bananas, blueberries, and yogurt in a blender. Add more milk if needed.*

3. *Start blending at a low speed and gradually increase the speed to high. Blend until the desired smoothness is reached.*

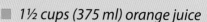
BREAKFAST OF CHIA-MPIONS

This smoothie provides lots of protein to kick start your day and keep you feeling full till lunchtime.

You Will Need:

- 2 cups (500 ml) coconut milk
- 1 tablespoon honey
- 1 cup (250 ml) old-fashioned rolled oats
- ¼ cup (60 ml) chia seeds
- 2 cups (500 ml) frozen or fresh strawberries

Makes 4 servings.

Rise and Shine
You Will Need: Ⓥ

- 1½ cups (375 ml) orange juice
- ¾ cup (180 ml) carrot juice
- 3 cups (750 ml) frozen mango chunks

Makes 4 servings.

Food for Thought

Can you spot four protein boosters (see below) in these recipes? What can you add to your favorite smoothie for a yummy protein boost? Try it and blend. (Answer on page 32.)

① Oats give this smoothie a thick and grainy feel. If you want a smoother feel, first put the oats in a blender and grind them until they look powdery. If not, skip this step.

② Put the coconut milk, honey, oats, chia seeds, and strawberries in a blender. Blend until the smoothie reaches desired smoothness.

③ Serve and sip at once. Otherwise, the consistency will become goopy as, over time, the chia seeds develop a jelly-like coating from being mixed with liquid.

SMOOTHIE PROTEIN BOOSTERS

Nuts Add up to ¼ cup (60 ml) of chopped nuts— almonds, cashews, walnuts, peanuts—per smoothie for a protein boost.

Oats Add ¼ cup (60 ml) per smoothie for a nutty-tasting protein boost.

Protein powder A variety of flavors, such as vanilla and chocolate, can power up your smoothies. Add a scoop per smoothie or the recommended amount on the package.

Seeds Chia seeds are a **complete protein** that provide **omega-3 fatty acids** without changing the flavor of a smoothie. Ground flaxseeds are rich in protein and omega-3 fatty acids and will add a slight nutty flavor. Add up to a ¼ cup (60 ml) per smoothie.

Tofu is made of soybeans— plants that have complete proteins. Silken tofu, also called soft or silk tofu—not regular tofu—gives smoothies a thick, creamy consistency and works well with fruit. Add up to ½ cup (125 ml) per smoothie.

Yogurt is a complete protein made of cow, goat, or sheep's milk. Add up to ½ cup (125 ml) per smoothie.

VEGETABLE SMOOTHIES

Whether they are thick as milkshakes, glowing lime green, or taste sweet beyond belief, green smoothies are a blend of leafy greens, fruit, and liquid. They are a tasty way to include more veggies in your healthy diet. Believe it or not, a whole carrot, or ½ cup (125 ml) of chopped broccoli or another veggie, counts as one serving of vegetables. (Same goes for fruit servings of a whole apple or orange or ½ cup [125 ml] of chopped fruit.) So you can figure out the number of servings you're drinking by adding up the veggie amounts in smoothie recipes and dividing the total by the number of smoothies a recipe makes.

THE GREAT BROWN GUZZLER

You Will Need:
- 2 large kale leaves
- 1 cup (250 ml) broccoli
- 1 carrot
- 2 apples
- ½ lemon
- 2 cups (500 ml) pomegranate juice
- 1 tablespoon (15 ml) ground flaxseed

Makes 4 servings.

If you want to boost your immune system or just chill out, this vitamin-filled green-brown smoothie rocks.

Wash and pat dry the kale. Remove the center ribs by tearing off the leaves.

Chop the broccoli into florets.

Peel the carrot, cut off both ends, and slice into chunks.

Core and peel the apples. Cut them into small chunks.

22

SWEET POTATO PIE SMOOTHIE

You Will Need:

- 2 cooked sweet potatoes
- 1 cup (250 ml) spinach
- 1 teaspoon (5 ml) pumpkin pie spice (ground cinnamon, ginger, nutmeg, allspice)
- 2 cups (500 ml) almond milk
- 1 teaspoon (5 ml) cinnamon
- 1 cup (250 ml) ice
- Optional: whip cream **V**

Makes 4 servings and keeps well in the fridge.

Even though it's made with sweet potato, this smoothie tastes just like pumpkin pie!

1. Peel, chop, and cook the sweet potatoes.

2. Wash the spinach and pat it dry.

3. If needed, make your own pumpkin pie spice. Mix 1 teaspoon (5 ml) ground cinnamon, ½ teaspoon (2 ml) ground ginger, ¼ teaspoon (1 ml) nutmeg, and ¼ teaspoon (1 ml) allspice in a container with a lid.

4. Put 1 cup (250 ml) almond milk, cinnamon, pumpkin pie spice, sweet potatoes, and spinach in the blender. Mix on high for about 30 seconds, so the ingredients are combined.

5. Add the remaining almond milk and ice and blend until the drink is smooth enough for you.

6. Top with whip cream and drink up!

Green Eggs and Beets

Is the food greener on the other side of the shelf? Huh? Sometimes, the word "green" refers to the way food is grown rather than its color. "Green," or organic, foods are grown without chemical fertilizers or pesticides. Organic farmers use renewable resources and methods that conserve soil and water for future generations. Next time you go to the grocery store, check out the organics on the other side of the shelf.

TRY THIS!

Red Planet in a Glass

You Will Need: **V**

- 1 cup (250 ml) carrot juice
- 1 cup (250 ml) apple juice
- 2 cups (500 ml) frozen pear chunks
- 1 small raw beet, peeled and thinly sliced
- 1 small apple, peeled and cored

Blend together. Makes 4 servings.

Peel the lemon and cut in half.

Put 1 cup (250 ml) of the pomegranate juice, ground flaxseed, broccoli, carrot, lemon, apple, and kale in a blender. Blend on low for about 30 seconds.

Add the remaining pomegranate juice and blend until the smoothie reaches your desired smoothness.

FRUIT SMOOTHIES

Feeling spent from racing your bestie, wiped from going all out in soccer, or just plain old tired? Give yourself an energy boost with a fruit smoothie. Fructose, a natural sugar found in fruit, makes fruit smoothies a natural energy drink. Fruits are also high in carbohydrates, which the body breaks down for energy. What's more, since you are drinking whole fruits in a smoothie, you're getting fiber that will help keep your digestive system on track.

PEACH MANGO TANGO

Let peaches and mangoes—a dynamite fruit combo—give you an energy boost that will wow your taste buds.

You Will Need:

- 2 cups (500 ml) milk
- 1 teaspoon (5 ml) vanilla extract
- 1 cup (250 ml) fresh or frozen mango chunks
- 1 cup (250 ml) fresh or frozen peach slices
- 1 fresh or frozen banana (If frozen, thaw banana for 5 minutes.)

Makes 4 servings.

Food for Thought

Strawberries and bananas go well together. Think about fruits you could combine with them, or come up with your own pair of fruits, to invent your own smoothie.

1 *Pour the milk and vanilla extract into a blender.*

2 *Add mango and peaches.*

3 *Peel the banana, slice it, or break it into chunks. Add it to the blender.*

BERRY BLASTER

Blast off with this triple-hit of berries. Don't be afraid to vary the berries. Any combination will be "berrilicious."

You Will Need:

- 1½ cups (375 ml) pomegranate juice
- ¾ (180 ml) cup water
- 1½ cups (375 ml) frozen strawberries
- ¾ cup (180 ml) frozen blueberries
- ¾ cup (180 ml) frozen raspberries
- ¾ cup (180 ml) frozen or fresh cherries

Makes 4 servings.

TRY THIS!

Pina Colada

You Will Need:

- 2 ½ cups (625 ml) coconut milk
- 3½ cups (875 ml) frozen pineapple chunks
- ¾ teaspoon (7 ml) coconut extract

Makes 4 servings.

The Grape Gr-appler

You Will Need:

- ¾ cup (180 ml) apple juice
- 2 apples, peeled and sliced
- ½ lemon, peeled and seeded
- 1 cup (250 ml) seedless red grapes

Makes 3 servings.

1 Pour the pomegranate juice and water into a blender.

2 Add strawberries, blueberries, raspberries, and cherries.

3 Blend until smooth.

4 Blend until desired smoothness is reached.

Food for Thought

Want to turn a smoothie into a popsicle? Pour it into an ice pop mold, freeze it, and break it out when you want to chill.

25

CHOCOLATE DELIGHT SMOOTHIES

Are you loco for cacao? If so, that's not bad, you know. Chocolate can help improve your memory and heart health. Studies show raw chocolate, called cacao, is loaded with fatty acids, fiber, potassium, magnesium, calcium, and antioxidants. Cacao's antioxidants play a part in healthy skin, help release natural pain and stress-fighting chemicals such as endorphins, and can even stop a case of diarrhea.

Food for Thought

Do you know the difference between cacao and cocoa? Find the answer on page 32.

LETTUCE CHOCOLATE DRINK

Lettuce? What lettuce? You won't be able to taste it in this smoothie. Plus, if you freeze it and eat it, you'll swear it's chocolate ice cream.

You Will Need:

- 2 cups (500 ml) almond milk
- 1 teaspoon (5 ml) vanilla extract
- 1 tablespoon (15 ml) cacao powder
- 2 bananas
- 1 cup (250 ml) Romaine lettuce
- Optional toppings: whip cream or topping, Smarties, chocolate chips or sprinkles

Makes 4 servings.

1. *Set aside 1 cup (250 ml) almond milk.*
2. *Put 1 cup almond milk, vanilla extract, and cacao powder in the blender.*
3. *Peel the bananas, break them in half, and add them to the blender.*
4. *Tear the lettuce into shreds and add it to the blender.*
5. *Blend the mixture until smooth.*
6. *Blend again. Open the blender lid and slowly add the almond milk that you set aside until the smoothie is smooth enough for you. Top with any of the optional toppings if you like.*

CHOCOLATE PEANUT BUTTER CUP

1. *Put the milk, cacao powder, and honey in a blender.*
2. *Peel the bananas, break them in half, and add them to the blender.*
3. *Blend until mixed. Add the peanut butter and blend again until you reach the desired level of smoothness.*

You Will Need:

- 2 cups (500 ml) milk
- 2 tablespoons (30 ml) cacao powder
- 2 tablespoons (30 ml) honey
- 2 tablespoons (30 ml) peanut butter
- 2 bananas

Makes 4 servings.

TIP

If you're allergic to peanut butter or looking for a change of taste, use almond butter, cashew butter, sunflower seed butter, pumpkin seed butter, or soynut butter instead.

COLD TREAT SMOOTHIES

Want to chill out with a frosty treat? Sorbet smoothies and smoothie bowls are guaranteed to hit the spot. Sorbet smoothies, and some smoothie bowls, are made with sherbet—a fruit drink. Smoothie bowls are thick smoothies poured into a bowl rather than a glass and topped with heaps of fresh and dried fruit, nuts, and seeds. They top up the liquid nutrients of a regular smoothie with more nutrients. Not only do you eat them with a spoon, but smoothie bowls also give you something to chew on—and then some. Is it any wonder they are nicknamed "cereal 2.0"?

MANGO MADNESS BOWL

A double-whammy of mango makes this a mouth-watering hit. If raspberries are in season, you can substitute the mango for raspberry sorbet and fresh raspberries.

1 Put the sorbet, yogurt, honey, coconut, and mango in a blender and blend until smooth.

2 For a thicker smoothie, add ice, one cube at time, and blend until the desired thickness is reached.

3 Pour into bowls and arrange desired toppings in rings on top.

You Will Need:
- 1½ cups (375 ml) mango sorbet
- ½ cup (125 ml) vanilla Greek yogurt
- 1 teaspoon (5 ml) liquid honey
- 1 cup (250 ml) frozen mango chunks
- 2 tablespoons (30 ml) unsweetened shredded coconut
- ice cubes (optional)
- Toppings: raspberries (or mango), unsweetened shredded coconut, granola, hemp seeds, ground flaxseed

Makes 4 servings.

BANANA SPLIT SUPREME

Looking for a special dessert or treat? Whip up this smoothie twist on the banana classic that tastes just like ice cream.

You Will Need:
- 1 cup (250 ml) milk
- 1 tablespoon (15 ml) honey
- 1 tablespoon (15 ml) cacao powder
- 2 frozen bananas (thawed 5 minutes)
- Optional: whipped cream or topping, chocolate chips, cherries or strawberries, pineapple, chopped peanuts or almonds, sliced fresh bananas

Makes 4 servings.

1 Put the milk, honey, and cacao powder in a blender.

2 Add the sliced frozen bananas and blend until desired smoothness is reached.

3 Pour into bowls.

4 Top with your favorite toppings and/or sliced fresh bananas if you like.

TRY THIS!

Kiwi Lime Koolio

You Will Need:
- ½ cup (125 ml) orange juice
- 3 tablespoons (45 ml) fresh lime juice
- 2 kiwis, peeled and sliced
- ¼ cup (60 ml) seedless green grapes
- ¼ cup (60 ml) lime sherbet

Blend together. Makes 2 smoothies.

Maple Fake Milkshake

You Will Need:
- 2 cups (500 ml) almond milk
- 2 frozen bananas
- 6 tablespoons (90 ml) maple syrup

Blend to make 4 servings.

VEGAN SMOOTHIES

Whether you're vegan, lactose intolerant, or just bored with plain old milk, there's a milk for you—almond, cashew, soy, coconut, and even rice milk. Even though they have less protein than cow's milk, they're often fortified with similar vitamins and minerals. They're similar in consistency to cow's milk too, except for cashew milk, which is thicker and creamier, and rice milk, which is thinner. Almond milk tastes slightly sweet and nutty, cashew milk tastes sweeter and less nutty, soy milk is slightly sweet, rice milk is sweet, and coconut milk tastes like coconut—what else? Give them a whirl.

THE GREEN MONSTER

You Will Need:

- 1 cup (250 ml) coconut milk
- 1 tablespoon (15 ml) chia seeds
- 2 bananas
- 3 cups (750 ml) spinach
- 1 packet stevia powder
- Optional: juice of 2 beets and ¼ cup (60 ml) maple syrup to make "beet blood"

Makes 2 servings.

Who knew drinking monster guts could be so delicious? This green smoothie is perfect for a monster bash, haunted house, or rainy day.

Peel and slice the bananas. If using frozen bananas, thaw the bananas slightly to soften them by letting them sit at room temperature for 5 minutes.

Put the coconut milk, stevia powder, chia seeds, bananas, and spinach in a blender and blend until smooth.

To make beet blood, use a spoon to mix the beet juice and maple syrup in a wide, shallow bowl. Dip the rim of a clear smoothie glass or cup in the beet blood.

Pour the green monster in the glass and watch the blood drip down sides of the glass.

ENERGIZER TONIC

Drink this high dose of nutrients and fiber to bring out your inner strength.

You Will Need:

- ⅓ cup (80 ml) of water
- 1 squirt of lemon juice
- ½ bunch asparagus
- ½ avocado
- 2 oranges, peeled
- 4 fresh basil leaves

Makes 1 serving.

Drink Pink to Think
You Will Need:

- 1 cup (250 ml) pomegranate juice
- ½ cup (125 ml) silken tofu
- 1 cup (250 ml) frozen blackberries

Makes 2 smoothies.

Berry "Broccolicious"
You Will Need:

- ¾ cup (180 ml) apple juice
- 2½ cups (625 ml) unsweetened vanilla almond or soy milk
- 3 cups (750 ml) mixed frozen berries
- 1 cup (250 ml) broccoli florets

Makes 4 servings.

1 Wash and chop the asparagus into small pieces.

2 Peel the oranges and separate into sections.

3 Add water and lemon juice to the blender.

4 Cut the avocado in half. Scoop out the flesh from one half into the blender.

Food for Thought

How many other vegan smoothies can you find in this book? How can you make one of your smoothie faves vegan? (Answers on page 32.)

5 Add the asparagus, oranges, and basil leaves on top and blend until smooth. If needed, add more water for a smoother smoothie.

LEARNING MORE

Books

The Help Yourself Cookbook for Kids: 60 Easy Plant-Based Recipes Kids Can Make to Stay Healthy and Save the Earth
by Ruby Roth, Andrews McMeel Publishing, 2016.

Smoothies for Kids
by Eliq Maranik, h.f.ullmann, 2016.

You're the Chef: Slurpable Smoothies/Drinks
by Kari Cornell, Lerner Publishing Group, 2013.

Websites

JuiceMaster
www.juicemaster.com/?s=smoothie
Juice & Smoothie Recipes for Kids at juicemaster.com.

AllRecipes
http://allrecipes.co.uk/recipes/tag-5685/kids-smoothie-recipes.aspx
Kids Smoothie Recipes at allrecipes.co.uk.

Kids Cooking Activities
www.kids-cooking-activities.com/simple-smoothie-recipes.html
Simple Smoothie Recipes at kids-cooking-actvities.com.

United States Department of Agriculture (USDA) Food Guide
www.choosemyplate.gov/MyPlate
U.S. guide to building a healthy eating style.

Canada Food Guide
www.hc-sc.gc.ca/fn-an/food-guide-aliment/choose-choix/index-eng.php
Eating well with Canada's Food Guide.

GLOSSARY

antioxidants Substances such as vitamin C that may prevent or delay some types of cell damage

carbohydrates One of the main types of nutrients found in food; converts to sugar in the digestive system which is used for energy for your cells, tissues, and organs

cholesterol A waxy, fat-like substance that occurs naturally in your body and is necessary in limited quantity for your body to work properly

complete protein Protein found in foods that come from animals, such as meat, poultry, fish, eggs, milk, and cheese; containing all the essential amino acids our bodies need

consistency The thickness of a liquid

enzyme A protein that speeds up, or controls, chemical reactions in the human body, such as those in digesting food

fiber Material found in fruits, vegetables, and whole-grain products that cannot be digested, but helps move food through the digestive system

flavonoids Substances found in fruits and vegetables that act as antioxidants

folate A type of B vitamin that helps make red blood cells and is found naturally in many foods such as vegetables, fruits, nuts, dairy products, meat, poultry, eggs, seafood, and grains

free radicals Substances that are necessary for cell development in low amounts, but at high amounts can damage cells and protein in the body

lactose A natural sugar found in milk

lactose intolerance A condition when a person cannot digest lactose easily

metabolism Chemical reactions within body's cells that convert the nutrients in food into the energy necessary to live

minerals Solid substances, such as iron, copper, and zinc, that the human body needs for good health and daily functions.

nutrients Substances, such as proteins, carbohydrates, fats, vitamins, and minerals, that provide nourishment essential for living things to grow and function

omega-3 fatty acid An essential fat that the body cannot make, but must get from other sources such as fish, nuts, flaxseeds, and leafy vegetables

pesticides Chemicals used on fruits and vegetables to kill pests, such as insects, to prevent them from harming and destroying crops

phytonutrients Chemicals found in fruits and vegetables that help prevent disease and keep your body working properly

protein Molecules that help build and repair cells in tissue such as muscle, bone, skin, and hair. They also power the body's chemical reactions and carry oxygen in your blood to your entire body.

vegan A person who does not eat or use products made from animals

vitamins Substances found in food that are essential to the growth and functioning of the human body

INDEX

FOOD FOR THOUGHT ANSWERS

Page 21

Question: Can you spot four protein boosters in these recipes? What can you add to your favorite smoothie for a yummy protein boost? Try it and blend.

Answer: Oats, chia seeds, yogurt, ground flaxseeds.

Page 29

Question 1: How many other vegan smoothies can you find in this book?

Answer 1: 17 smoothies

Question 2: How can you make one of your smoothie faves vegan?

Answer 2: Substitute almond milk, cashew milk, soy milk, rice milk, or coconut milk for cow's milk.

Page 26

Question: Do you know the difference between cacao and cocoa?

Answer: The words "cacao" and "cocoa" both come from "cacahuatl," an Aztec word for the cacao plant, which grows in areas close to the equator. Each cacao tree produces pods from its trunk that look like small pumpkins. Inside each pod are 50 or more small cacao beans that look like coffee beans. The harvested beans are turned into two types of product. One is raw cacao, which can be pressed into cacao powder. The other is cocoa, which is made by roasting the beans at high temperatures and grinding them into a powder. Cacao contains more healthful nutrients because it is not highly processed, but cocoa is still a good source of fiber and antioxidants. Either one can be used in baking and cooking.